50 Kids Can Cook Recipes for Home

By: Kelly Johnson

Table of Contents

- Mini Pizzas
- Fruit Kabobs
- Peanut Butter Banana Sandwiches
- DIY Tacos
- Cheesy Quesadillas
- Veggie Wraps
- Pasta Salad
- Homemade Trail Mix
- Breakfast Burritos
- Chocolate Dipped Strawberries
- Rainbow Smoothies
- No-Bake Energy Bites
- Mini Pancake Stacks
- Apple Nachos
- Oven-Baked Chicken Nuggets
- Homemade Pizza Rolls
- Caprese Skewers
- Vegetable Stir-Fry
- Fruit Smoothie Bowls
- S'mores Dip
- Easy Macaroni and Cheese
- Zucchini Fritters
- Yogurt Parfaits
- Homemade Popsicles
- Cereal Treats
- Stuffed Peppers
- Vegetable Soup
- Oven-Baked Sweet Potato Fries
- Cheesy Garlic Bread
- Chocolate Chip Cookies
- Mini Meatloaves
- Tortilla Roll-Ups
- Baked Oatmeal Cups
- Pasta with Marinara Sauce

- Fruit and Yogurt Cups
- Muffin Tin Omelets
- Rice Krispie Treats
- Easy Fried Rice
- Potato Skins
- Spaghetti and Meatballs
- Corn on the Cob
- Egg Salad Sandwiches
- Cucumber Sandwiches
- Homemade Hummus and Veggies
- Chocolate Mug Cake
- Rainbow Veggie Pizza
- Mini Frittatas
- Taco Salad
- Homemade Sliders
- Nut Butter and Apple Slices

Mini Pizzas

Ingredients

- 1 package English muffins or mini pizza crusts
- 1 cup pizza sauce
- 1 cup shredded mozzarella cheese
- Assorted toppings (pepperoni, bell peppers, olives, etc.)

Instructions

1. **Preheat Oven:** Preheat your oven to 375°F (190°C).
2. **Assemble Pizzas:** Split the English muffins in half and place them on a baking sheet. Spread pizza sauce on each half, top with cheese, and add desired toppings.
3. **Bake:** Bake for 10-15 minutes, or until the cheese is melted and bubbly.
4. **Serve:** Let cool slightly before serving. Enjoy!

Fruit Kabobs

Ingredients

- Assorted fruits (strawberries, grapes, pineapple, melon, etc.)
- Skewers or toothpicks
- Optional: yogurt or chocolate for dipping

Instructions

1. **Prepare Fruit:** Wash and cut fruits into bite-sized pieces.
2. **Assemble Kabobs:** Thread pieces of fruit onto skewers in an alternating pattern.
3. **Serve:** Serve as is or with yogurt or chocolate for dipping. Enjoy!

Peanut Butter Banana Sandwiches

Ingredients

- 2 slices of bread (whole grain or white)
- 2 tablespoons peanut butter
- 1 banana, sliced
- Honey (optional)

Instructions

1. **Spread Peanut Butter:** Spread peanut butter evenly on one slice of bread.
2. **Add Banana:** Layer banana slices on top of the peanut butter. Drizzle with honey if desired.
3. **Top and Cut:** Place the other slice of bread on top, press down gently, and cut into halves or quarters.
4. **Serve:** Enjoy immediately!

DIY Tacos

Ingredients

- 1 lb ground beef or turkey (or beans for a vegetarian option)
- 1 packet taco seasoning
- Taco shells or tortillas
- Assorted toppings (lettuce, tomato, cheese, sour cream, salsa, etc.)

Instructions

1. **Cook Meat:** In a skillet, cook ground meat until browned. Drain excess fat, then add taco seasoning and follow packet instructions.
2. **Assemble Tacos:** Fill taco shells or tortillas with meat and top with desired toppings.
3. **Serve:** Enjoy immediately!

Cheesy Quesadillas

Ingredients

- 2 flour tortillas
- 1 cup shredded cheese (cheddar, mozzarella, or Mexican blend)
- Optional: cooked chicken, beans, or veggies

Instructions

1. **Heat Pan:** Heat a skillet over medium heat.
2. **Assemble Quesadilla:** Place one tortilla in the skillet, sprinkle cheese evenly, and add optional fillings. Top with the second tortilla.
3. **Cook:** Cook for 3-4 minutes on each side, or until cheese is melted and tortillas are golden.
4. **Serve:** Cut into wedges and enjoy with salsa or sour cream!

Veggie Wraps

Ingredients

- 1 large tortilla or wrap
- 2 tablespoons hummus or cream cheese
- Assorted veggies (cucumber, bell pepper, carrots, spinach, etc.)
- Optional: sliced turkey or cheese

Instructions

1. **Spread Filling:** Spread hummus or cream cheese evenly over the tortilla.
2. **Add Veggies:** Layer assorted veggies (and optional turkey or cheese) in the center of the tortilla.
3. **Wrap:** Roll the tortilla tightly, tucking in the sides as you go.
4. **Serve:** Slice in half and enjoy!

Pasta Salad

Ingredients

- 2 cups cooked pasta (any shape)
- 1 cup cherry tomatoes, halved
- 1 cucumber, diced
- ½ cup bell pepper, diced
- ½ cup olives (optional)
- ½ cup Italian dressing

Instructions

1. **Combine Ingredients:** In a large bowl, combine cooked pasta, cherry tomatoes, cucumber, bell pepper, and olives.
2. **Add Dressing:** Pour Italian dressing over the salad and toss to coat.
3. **Chill:** Refrigerate for at least 30 minutes before serving.
4. **Serve:** Enjoy cold!

Homemade Trail Mix

Ingredients

- 1 cup mixed nuts (almonds, walnuts, cashews)
- 1 cup dried fruit (raisins, cranberries, apricots)
- 1 cup chocolate chips or M&Ms
- 1 cup seeds (pumpkin or sunflower)
- Optional: coconut flakes or pretzels

Instructions

1. **Combine Ingredients:** In a large bowl, mix together all ingredients.
2. **Store:** Store in an airtight container or zip-top bag.
3. **Serve:** Enjoy as a snack!

Breakfast Burritos

Ingredients

- 4 large tortillas
- 6 large eggs
- 1 cup cooked sausage or bacon, crumbled
- 1 cup shredded cheese (cheddar or Monterey Jack)
- ½ cup diced bell peppers and onions
- Salt and pepper to taste

Instructions

1. **Scramble Eggs:** In a skillet, scramble eggs with bell peppers and onions; season with salt and pepper.
2. **Assemble Burritos:** Lay a tortilla flat, add scrambled eggs, meat, and cheese, then roll tightly.
3. **Cook (Optional):** For crispy burritos, place seam-side down in a skillet over medium heat for 2-3 minutes per side.
4. **Serve:** Enjoy warm!

Chocolate Dipped Strawberries

Ingredients

- 1 lb fresh strawberries, washed and dried
- 1 cup chocolate chips (dark or milk)
- Optional: sprinkles or crushed nuts for decoration

Instructions

1. **Melt Chocolate:** In a microwave-safe bowl, melt chocolate chips in 30-second intervals, stirring until smooth.
2. **Dip Strawberries:** Dip each strawberry into melted chocolate, allowing excess to drip off.
3. **Decorate (Optional):** Sprinkle with toppings if desired.
4. **Set:** Place dipped strawberries on a parchment-lined baking sheet and refrigerate until chocolate hardens.
5. **Serve:** Enjoy chilled!

Rainbow Smoothies

Ingredients

- 1 cup spinach
- 1 banana
- 1 cup pineapple chunks
- 1 cup strawberries
- 1 cup yogurt or milk (for blending)
- Optional: honey or agave syrup

Instructions

1. **Blend Green Layer:** Blend spinach, banana, and half of the yogurt/milk until smooth. Pour into glasses and freeze for 15 minutes.
2. **Blend Yellow Layer:** Blend pineapple with the remaining yogurt/milk until smooth. Pour gently over the green layer. Freeze for 15 minutes.
3. **Blend Red Layer:** Blend strawberries with honey or syrup until smooth. Pour gently over the yellow layer.
4. **Serve:** Enjoy immediately with a straw!

No-Bake Energy Bites

Ingredients

- 1 cup rolled oats
- ½ cup peanut butter
- ⅓ cup honey
- ½ cup chocolate chips
- ¼ cup chia seeds or flaxseeds

Instructions

1. **Mix Ingredients:** In a bowl, combine all ingredients and mix until well combined.
2. **Form Bites:** Roll the mixture into small balls, about 1 inch in diameter.
3. **Chill:** Place energy bites in the refrigerator for 30 minutes to set.
4. **Serve:** Enjoy as a quick snack!

Mini Pancake Stacks

Ingredients

- 1 cup pancake mix
- ¾ cup milk
- 1 egg
- Maple syrup and fruit for serving

Instructions

1. **Prepare Pancake Batter:** In a bowl, mix pancake mix, milk, and egg until combined.
2. **Cook Pancakes:** Heat a non-stick skillet over medium heat. Pour small amounts of batter (about 2 tablespoons) to form mini pancakes. Cook until bubbles form, then flip and cook until golden.
3. **Stack and Serve:** Stack pancakes and drizzle with maple syrup and fruit. Enjoy!

Apple Nachos

Ingredients

- 2 large apples, sliced
- ½ cup peanut butter or almond butter
- ¼ cup granola
- ¼ cup chocolate chips or drizzle
- Optional: shredded coconut or chopped nuts

Instructions

1. **Arrange Apples:** Arrange apple slices on a plate or platter.
2. **Drizzle and Top:** Drizzle with peanut butter, then sprinkle with granola and chocolate chips.
3. **Serve:** Enjoy immediately as a fun snack!

Oven-Baked Chicken Nuggets

Ingredients

- 1 lb chicken breast, cut into bite-sized pieces
- 1 cup breadcrumbs (panko or regular)
- ½ cup grated Parmesan cheese
- 1 teaspoon garlic powder
- 1 teaspoon paprika
- Salt and pepper to taste
- 2 large eggs, beaten

Instructions

1. **Preheat Oven:** Preheat your oven to 400°F (200°C) and line a baking sheet with parchment paper.
2. **Mix Coating:** In a bowl, combine breadcrumbs, Parmesan, garlic powder, paprika, salt, and pepper.
3. **Coat Chicken:** Dip chicken pieces in beaten eggs, then coat in the breadcrumb mixture.
4. **Arrange and Bake:** Place coated nuggets on the prepared baking sheet and bake for 15-20 minutes, or until golden and cooked through.
5. **Serve:** Enjoy with your favorite dipping sauce!

Homemade Pizza Rolls

Ingredients

- 1 package pizza dough (store-bought or homemade)
- 1 cup pizza sauce
- 1 cup shredded mozzarella cheese
- Assorted toppings (pepperoni, bell peppers, olives, etc.)
- Olive oil for brushing

Instructions

1. **Preheat Oven:** Preheat your oven to 400°F (200°C) and line a baking sheet with parchment paper.
2. **Roll Out Dough:** Roll out the pizza dough into a rectangle about ¼ inch thick.
3. **Assemble:** Spread pizza sauce over the dough, sprinkle cheese and toppings evenly.
4. **Roll and Cut:** Roll the dough tightly into a log and slice into 1-inch pieces.
5. **Bake:** Place rolls on the baking sheet, brush with olive oil, and bake for 15-20 minutes, or until golden.
6. **Serve:** Enjoy warm with extra pizza sauce for dipping!

Caprese Skewers

Ingredients

- 1 pint cherry tomatoes
- 8 oz fresh mozzarella balls
- Fresh basil leaves
- Balsamic glaze for drizzling
- Salt and pepper to taste

Instructions

1. **Assemble Skewers:** On small skewers or toothpicks, thread a cherry tomato, a basil leaf, and a mozzarella ball. Repeat until all ingredients are used.
2. **Season:** Drizzle with balsamic glaze and sprinkle with salt and pepper.
3. **Serve:** Enjoy as a fresh appetizer or snack!

Vegetable Stir-Fry

Ingredients

- 2 cups mixed vegetables (bell peppers, broccoli, carrots, snap peas, etc.)
- 2 tablespoons soy sauce
- 1 tablespoon olive oil
- 1 teaspoon minced garlic
- 1 teaspoon grated ginger (optional)

Instructions

1. **Heat Oil:** In a large skillet or wok, heat olive oil over medium-high heat.
2. **Add Veggies:** Add garlic and ginger, sautéing for 30 seconds before adding mixed vegetables.
3. **Stir-Fry:** Stir-fry for 5-7 minutes, or until vegetables are tender but still crisp.
4. **Add Sauce:** Pour in soy sauce and stir to coat. Cook for another minute.
5. **Serve:** Enjoy hot over rice or noodles!

Fruit Smoothie Bowls

Ingredients

- 2 bananas, frozen
- 1 cup mixed berries (frozen or fresh)
- 1 cup yogurt or milk
- Toppings: granola, sliced fruit, nuts, seeds, coconut flakes

Instructions

1. **Blend Base:** In a blender, combine frozen bananas, berries, and yogurt/milk until smooth.
2. **Pour:** Pour the smoothie mixture into bowls.
3. **Add Toppings:** Top with granola, sliced fruit, nuts, and other toppings of your choice.
4. **Serve:** Enjoy immediately with a spoon!

S'mores Dip

Ingredients

- 1 cup chocolate chips (milk or dark)
- 1 cup mini marshmallows
- 1 tablespoon graham cracker crumbs
- Graham crackers for dipping

Instructions

1. **Preheat Oven:** Preheat your oven to 350°F (175°C) and prepare a small baking dish.
2. **Layer Ingredients:** Spread chocolate chips in the bottom of the dish, then top with mini marshmallows and graham cracker crumbs.
3. **Bake:** Bake for 10-12 minutes, or until marshmallows are golden and chocolate is melted.
4. **Serve:** Enjoy warm with graham crackers for dipping!

Easy Macaroni and Cheese

Ingredients

- 2 cups elbow macaroni
- 2 tablespoons butter
- 2 tablespoons all-purpose flour
- 2 cups milk
- 2 cups shredded cheddar cheese
- Salt and pepper to taste

Instructions

1. **Cook Pasta:** Cook macaroni according to package instructions; drain and set aside.
2. **Make Sauce:** In a saucepan, melt butter over medium heat. Stir in flour and cook for 1 minute. Gradually whisk in milk, cooking until thickened.
3. **Add Cheese:** Remove from heat and stir in cheese until melted. Season with salt and pepper.
4. **Combine:** Add cooked macaroni to the cheese sauce and mix well.
5. **Serve:** Enjoy warm!

Zucchini Fritters

Ingredients

- 2 medium zucchinis, grated
- 1 cup breadcrumbs
- 1 large egg
- ½ cup grated Parmesan cheese
- 2 cloves garlic, minced
- Salt and pepper to taste
- Olive oil for frying

Instructions

1. **Prepare Zucchini:** Squeeze grated zucchini in a clean kitchen towel to remove excess moisture.
2. **Mix Ingredients:** In a bowl, combine zucchini, breadcrumbs, egg, Parmesan, garlic, salt, and pepper.
3. **Form Fritters:** Heat olive oil in a skillet over medium heat. Form the mixture into patties and cook for 3-4 minutes per side, until golden brown.
4. **Serve:** Enjoy warm with dipping sauce or plain!

Yogurt Parfaits

Ingredients

- 2 cups yogurt (any flavor)
- 1 cup granola
- 1 cup mixed berries (strawberries, blueberries, raspberries)
- Honey or maple syrup (optional)

Instructions

1. **Layer Ingredients:** In glasses or bowls, layer yogurt, granola, and mixed berries.
2. **Repeat Layers:** Continue layering until ingredients are used, finishing with berries on top.
3. **Drizzle:** Drizzle with honey or syrup if desired.
4. **Serve:** Enjoy immediately!

Homemade Popsicles

Ingredients

- 2 cups fruit juice (or blended fruit)
- 1 cup yogurt (optional for creaminess)
- Fresh fruit pieces (optional)
  Instructions
1. **Mix Ingredients:** In a bowl, combine fruit juice and yogurt (if using).
2. **Fill Molds:** Pour the mixture into popsicle molds, adding fresh fruit pieces if desired.
3. **Freeze:** Insert sticks and freeze for at least 4-6 hours or until solid.
4. **Serve:** Run molds under warm water to release popsicles. Enjoy!

Cereal Treats

Ingredients

- 4 cups crispy rice cereal
- 1 cup mini marshmallows
- ¼ cup butter
- ½ teaspoon vanilla extract

Instructions

1. **Melt Ingredients:** In a large saucepan, melt butter over low heat. Add marshmallows and stir until melted and smooth. Remove from heat and stir in vanilla.
2. **Combine with Cereal:** Add crispy rice cereal to the marshmallow mixture and stir until evenly coated.
3. **Press into Pan:** Pour mixture into a greased 9x13-inch baking dish and press down firmly.
4. **Cool and Cut:** Let cool for about 30 minutes, then cut into squares. Enjoy!

Stuffed Peppers

Ingredients

- 4 bell peppers (any color)
- 1 lb ground beef or turkey
- 1 cup cooked rice
- 1 cup diced tomatoes (canned or fresh)
- 1 teaspoon Italian seasoning
- 1 cup shredded cheese (optional)

Instructions

1. **Preheat Oven:** Preheat your oven to 375°F (190°C).
2. **Cook Filling:** In a skillet, cook ground meat until browned. Stir in cooked rice, diced tomatoes, and Italian seasoning.
3. **Prepare Peppers:** Cut the tops off the bell peppers and remove seeds. Stuff with the meat mixture.
4. **Bake:** Place stuffed peppers in a baking dish, cover with foil, and bake for 30 minutes. If using cheese, uncover and sprinkle on top, baking for an additional 10 minutes.
5. **Serve:** Enjoy warm!

Vegetable Soup

Ingredients

- 4 cups vegetable broth
- 1 cup diced carrots
- 1 cup diced celery
- 1 cup diced potatoes
- 1 can diced tomatoes (14 oz)
- 1 teaspoon dried thyme
- Salt and pepper to taste

Instructions

1. **Combine Ingredients:** In a large pot, combine vegetable broth, carrots, celery, potatoes, diced tomatoes, thyme, salt, and pepper.
2. **Simmer:** Bring to a boil, then reduce heat and simmer for 20-30 minutes, or until vegetables are tender.
3. **Serve:** Enjoy warm with crusty bread!

Oven-Baked Sweet Potato Fries

Ingredients

- 2 large sweet potatoes, cut into fries
- 2 tablespoons olive oil
- 1 teaspoon paprika
- ½ teaspoon garlic powder
- Salt and pepper to taste

Instructions

1. **Preheat Oven:** Preheat your oven to 425°F (220°C) and line a baking sheet with parchment paper.
2. **Season Fries:** In a large bowl, toss sweet potato fries with olive oil, paprika, garlic powder, salt, and pepper until evenly coated.
3. **Bake:** Spread fries in a single layer on the baking sheet and bake for 20-25 minutes, flipping halfway, until crispy and golden.
4. **Serve:** Enjoy hot with your favorite dipping sauce!

Cheesy Garlic Bread

Ingredients

- 1 loaf French bread or Italian bread
- ½ cup butter, softened
- 2 cloves garlic, minced
- 1 cup shredded mozzarella cheese
- ¼ cup grated Parmesan cheese
- 1 tablespoon chopped parsley (optional)

Instructions

1. **Preheat Oven:** Preheat your oven to 375°F (190°C).
2. **Mix Topping:** In a bowl, combine softened butter, minced garlic, mozzarella, Parmesan, and parsley.
3. **Prepare Bread:** Slice the bread in half lengthwise and spread the garlic mixture evenly over both halves.
4. **Bake:** Place on a baking sheet and bake for 10-15 minutes, or until the cheese is melted and bubbly.
5. **Serve:** Slice and enjoy warm!

Chocolate Chip Cookies

Ingredients

- 1 cup butter, softened
- ¾ cup granulated sugar
- ¾ cup brown sugar
- 1 teaspoon vanilla extract
- 2 large eggs
- 2 ¼ cups all-purpose flour
- 1 teaspoon baking soda
- ½ teaspoon salt
- 2 cups chocolate chips

Instructions

1. **Preheat Oven:** Preheat your oven to 350°F (175°C).
2. **Cream Ingredients:** In a large bowl, cream together butter, granulated sugar, brown sugar, and vanilla. Beat in eggs one at a time.
3. **Combine Dry Ingredients:** In another bowl, whisk together flour, baking soda, and salt. Gradually add to the creamed mixture.
4. **Add Chocolate Chips:** Stir in chocolate chips.
5. **Bake Cookies:** Drop spoonfuls of dough onto a baking sheet and bake for 10-12 minutes, or until golden.
6. **Serve:** Let cool slightly before enjoying!

Mini Meatloaves

Ingredients

- 1 lb ground beef or turkey
- 1 cup breadcrumbs
- 1 egg
- ½ cup milk
- ½ cup ketchup
- 1 teaspoon garlic powder
- Salt and pepper to taste

Instructions

1. **Preheat Oven:** Preheat your oven to 350°F (175°C) and lightly grease a muffin tin.
2. **Mix Ingredients:** In a large bowl, combine ground meat, breadcrumbs, egg, milk, ¼ cup ketchup, garlic powder, salt, and pepper.
3. **Form Mini Loaves:** Divide the mixture evenly among the muffin tin cups, pressing down slightly.
4. **Top and Bake:** Spread remaining ketchup on top of each mini meatloaf. Bake for 25-30 minutes, or until cooked through.
5. **Serve:** Enjoy warm!

Tortilla Roll-Ups

Ingredients

- 4 large tortillas
- 1 cup cream cheese, softened
- 1 cup deli meats (ham, turkey, or chicken)
- 1 cup shredded cheese
- Assorted veggies (spinach, bell peppers, cucumbers)

Instructions

1. **Spread Cream Cheese:** Spread cream cheese evenly over each tortilla.
2. **Layer Ingredients:** Layer deli meats, shredded cheese, and veggies on top of the cream cheese.
3. **Roll and Slice:** Roll up tightly, then slice into bite-sized pieces.
4. **Serve:** Enjoy as a quick snack or appetizer!

Baked Oatmeal Cups

Ingredients

- 2 cups rolled oats
- 1 teaspoon baking powder
- ½ teaspoon cinnamon
- ¼ teaspoon salt
- 2 cups milk
- 2 large eggs
- ¼ cup honey or maple syrup
- 1 cup mixed berries (fresh or frozen)

Instructions

1. **Preheat Oven:** Preheat your oven to 350°F (175°C) and grease a muffin tin.
2. **Mix Dry Ingredients:** In a bowl, combine oats, baking powder, cinnamon, and salt.
3. **Combine Wet Ingredients:** In another bowl, whisk together milk, eggs, and honey.
4. **Combine Mixtures:** Add the wet mixture to the dry ingredients and stir in berries.
5. **Bake:** Pour the mixture into muffin cups, filling each about ¾ full. Bake for 20-25 minutes, or until set.
6. **Serve:** Enjoy warm or at room temperature!

Pasta with Marinara Sauce

Ingredients

- 8 oz pasta (spaghetti, penne, etc.)
- 2 cups marinara sauce
- 1 tablespoon olive oil
- 1 teaspoon Italian seasoning
- Grated Parmesan cheese for serving

Instructions

1. **Cook Pasta:** Cook pasta according to package instructions; drain and set aside.
2. **Heat Sauce:** In a saucepan, heat marinara sauce with olive oil and Italian seasoning until warmed through.
3. **Combine:** Add cooked pasta to the sauce and toss to combine.
4. **Serve:** Serve hot, topped with grated Parmesan cheese. Enjoy!

Fruit and Yogurt Cups

Ingredients

- 2 cups yogurt (any flavor)
- 2 cups mixed fresh fruit (berries, bananas, peaches, etc.)
- ½ cup granola
- Honey or maple syrup (optional)

Instructions

1. **Layer Ingredients:** In cups or bowls, layer yogurt, mixed fruit, and granola.
2. **Repeat Layers:** Continue layering until ingredients are used up.
3. **Drizzle (Optional):** Drizzle with honey or syrup if desired.
4. **Serve:** Enjoy immediately!

Muffin Tin Omelets

Ingredients

- 6 large eggs
- ½ cup milk
- 1 cup diced vegetables (bell peppers, spinach, onions, etc.)
- 1 cup shredded cheese (cheddar or mozzarella)
- Salt and pepper to taste

Instructions

1. **Preheat Oven:** Preheat your oven to 350°F (175°C) and grease a muffin tin.
2. **Whisk Eggs:** In a bowl, whisk together eggs, milk, salt, and pepper.
3. **Add Fillings:** Divide the vegetables and cheese evenly among the muffin cups.
4. **Pour Egg Mixture:** Pour the egg mixture over the fillings, filling each cup about ¾ full.
5. **Bake:** Bake for 20-25 minutes, or until the eggs are set.
6. **Serve:** Enjoy warm!

Rice Krispie Treats

Ingredients

- 3 tablespoons butter
- 1 package (10 oz) mini marshmallows
- 6 cups Rice Krispies cereal

Instructions

1. **Melt Butter:** In a large saucepan, melt butter over low heat.
2. **Add Marshmallows:** Stir in marshmallows and continue to cook until melted and smooth.
3. **Mix in Cereal:** Remove from heat and add Rice Krispies, stirring until well coated.
4. **Press into Pan:** Pour the mixture into a greased 9x13-inch baking dish and press down firmly.
5. **Cool and Cut:** Allow to cool before cutting into squares. Enjoy!

Easy Fried Rice

Ingredients

- 2 cups cooked rice (preferably cold)
- 2 tablespoons vegetable oil
- 2 eggs, beaten
- 1 cup mixed vegetables (peas, carrots, corn)
- 2 tablespoons soy sauce
- Green onions for garnish (optional)

Instructions

1. **Heat Oil:** In a large skillet or wok, heat vegetable oil over medium heat.
2. **Cook Eggs:** Add beaten eggs and scramble until fully cooked; remove from skillet.
3. **Stir-Fry Veggies:** In the same skillet, add mixed vegetables and stir-fry for 2-3 minutes.
4. **Add Rice:** Add cooked rice and soy sauce, stirring to combine. Return scrambled eggs to the skillet and mix well.
5. **Serve:** Garnish with green onions if desired and enjoy!

Potato Skins

Ingredients

- 4 large russet potatoes
- 1 cup shredded cheese (cheddar or your choice)
- ½ cup cooked bacon, crumbled
- ¼ cup sour cream
- Chopped green onions for garnish

Instructions

1. **Preheat Oven:** Preheat your oven to 400°F (200°C).
2. **Bake Potatoes:** Bake potatoes for about 45 minutes, or until tender. Allow to cool slightly.
3. **Scoop and Prepare:** Cut potatoes in half and scoop out some flesh, leaving a thin layer.
4. **Fill and Bake:** Place skins on a baking sheet, fill with cheese and bacon, and return to the oven for 10-15 minutes, or until cheese is melted.
5. **Serve:** Top with sour cream and green onions before enjoying!

Spaghetti and Meatballs

Ingredients

- 8 oz spaghetti
- 1 lb ground beef or turkey
- 1 cup breadcrumbs
- 1 egg
- 1 cup marinara sauce
- 1 teaspoon Italian seasoning
- Salt and pepper to taste

Instructions

1. **Cook Pasta:** Cook spaghetti according to package instructions; drain and set aside.
2. **Prepare Meatballs:** In a bowl, combine ground meat, breadcrumbs, egg, Italian seasoning, salt, and pepper. Form into meatballs.
3. **Cook Meatballs:** In a skillet, brown meatballs on all sides, then add marinara sauce and simmer for 10-15 minutes.
4. **Combine and Serve:** Toss cooked spaghetti with sauce and meatballs. Enjoy hot!

Corn on the Cob

Ingredients

- 4 ears of corn, husked
- Butter, for serving
- Salt, for serving

Instructions

1. **Boil Corn:** Bring a large pot of water to a boil. Add corn and cook for 5-7 minutes, or until tender.
2. **Drain:** Remove corn from the pot and let cool slightly.
3. **Serve:** Spread with butter and sprinkle with salt before enjoying!

Egg Salad Sandwiches

Ingredients

- 6 hard-boiled eggs, chopped
- ¼ cup mayonnaise
- 1 teaspoon Dijon mustard
- 1 tablespoon chopped fresh dill (or parsley)
- Salt and pepper to taste
- Bread (whole grain, white, or your choice)

Instructions

1. **Mix Ingredients:** In a bowl, combine chopped eggs, mayonnaise, Dijon mustard, dill, salt, and pepper. Mix until well combined.
2. **Assemble Sandwiches:** Spread the egg salad onto slices of bread. Top with another slice to form a sandwich.
3. **Serve:** Cut into halves or quarters and enjoy!

Cucumber Sandwiches

Ingredients

- 1 large cucumber, thinly sliced
- 8 oz cream cheese, softened
- 1 tablespoon fresh dill (or chives)
- Salt and pepper to taste
- Bread (white or whole grain)
Instructions
1. **Prepare Cream Cheese:** In a bowl, mix softened cream cheese with dill, salt, and pepper.
2. **Assemble Sandwiches:** Spread cream cheese mixture on slices of bread. Top with cucumber slices and another slice of bread.
3. **Serve:** Cut into triangles or quarters and enjoy!

Homemade Hummus and Veggies

Ingredients

- 1 can (15 oz) chickpeas, drained and rinsed
- ¼ cup tahini
- 2 tablespoons olive oil
- 2 tablespoons lemon juice
- 1 garlic clove, minced
- Salt to taste
- Assorted vegetables (carrots, bell peppers, celery) for dipping

Instructions

1. **Blend Ingredients:** In a food processor, combine chickpeas, tahini, olive oil, lemon juice, garlic, and salt. Blend until smooth.
2. **Adjust Consistency:** If too thick, add water 1 tablespoon at a time until desired consistency is reached.
3. **Serve:** Transfer hummus to a bowl and serve with assorted vegetables for dipping!

Chocolate Mug Cake

Ingredients

- 4 tablespoons all-purpose flour
- 4 tablespoons sugar
- 2 tablespoons cocoa powder
- 1/8 teaspoon baking powder
- 3 tablespoons milk
- 2 tablespoons vegetable oil
- 1/4 teaspoon vanilla extract
- A pinch of salt

Instructions

1. **Mix Dry Ingredients:** In a microwave-safe mug, combine flour, sugar, cocoa powder, baking powder, and salt.
2. **Add Wet Ingredients:** Stir in milk, vegetable oil, and vanilla extract until smooth.
3. **Microwave:** Microwave on high for 1 minute to 1 minute 30 seconds, or until the cake is cooked through.
4. **Serve:** Let cool slightly before enjoying straight from the mug!

Rainbow Veggie Pizza

Ingredients

- 1 pre-made pizza crust (or flatbread)
- ½ cup pizza sauce
- 1 cup shredded mozzarella cheese
- Assorted colorful veggies (bell peppers, cherry tomatoes, spinach, red onion, etc.)
- Olive oil for drizzling

Instructions

1. **Preheat Oven:** Preheat your oven according to pizza crust instructions.
2. **Assemble Pizza:** Spread pizza sauce over the crust, then sprinkle with cheese. Arrange veggies in a rainbow pattern on top.
3. **Bake:** Bake according to crust instructions, usually about 10-15 minutes, or until cheese is melted and bubbly.
4. **Serve:** Drizzle with olive oil and enjoy warm!

Mini Frittatas

Ingredients

- 6 large eggs
- ½ cup milk
- 1 cup diced vegetables (bell peppers, spinach, onions, etc.)
- ½ cup shredded cheese (cheddar or your choice)
- Salt and pepper to taste

Instructions

1. **Preheat Oven:** Preheat your oven to 350°F (175°C) and grease a muffin tin.
2. **Whisk Eggs:** In a bowl, whisk together eggs, milk, salt, and pepper.
3. **Add Fillings:** Divide the diced vegetables and cheese evenly among the muffin cups.
4. **Pour Egg Mixture:** Pour the egg mixture over the fillings, filling each cup about ¾ full.
5. **Bake:** Bake for 20-25 minutes, or until the eggs are set and lightly golden.
6. **Serve:** Enjoy warm or at room temperature!

Taco Salad

Ingredients

- 1 lb ground beef or turkey
- 1 packet taco seasoning
- 6 cups chopped romaine lettuce
- 1 cup diced tomatoes
- 1 cup canned black beans, rinsed and drained
- 1 cup corn (fresh, canned, or frozen)
- 1 cup shredded cheese (cheddar or Mexican blend)
- Tortilla chips for serving
- Salsa and sour cream for topping (optional)

Instructions

1. **Cook Meat:** In a skillet, cook ground meat until browned. Stir in taco seasoning and water according to package instructions.
2. **Assemble Salad:** In a large bowl, combine lettuce, tomatoes, black beans, corn, and cheese.
3. **Add Meat:** Top the salad with the cooked taco meat.
4. **Serve:** Serve with tortilla chips and optional toppings like salsa and sour cream. Enjoy!

Homemade Sliders

Ingredients

- 1 lb ground beef or turkey
- 1 teaspoon garlic powder
- 1 teaspoon onion powder
- Salt and pepper to taste
- 12 small slider buns
- Cheese slices (optional)
- Lettuce, tomato, and condiments for serving

Instructions

1. **Preheat Oven:** Preheat your oven to 350°F (175°C).
2. **Mix Ingredients:** In a bowl, combine ground meat, garlic powder, onion powder, salt, and pepper. Form into small patties.
3. **Cook Patties:** In a skillet, cook patties over medium heat until browned and cooked through, about 3-4 minutes per side. If using cheese, place on patties during the last minute of cooking to melt.
4. **Assemble Sliders:** Place cooked patties on slider buns and top with lettuce, tomato, and your favorite condiments.
5. **Serve:** Enjoy warm!

Nut Butter and Apple Slices

Ingredients

- 2 large apples, sliced
- ½ cup nut butter (peanut, almond, or your choice)
- Optional toppings: granola, raisins, or cinnamon
  Instructions
1. **Prepare Apple Slices:** Wash and slice apples into wedges.
2. **Spread Nut Butter:** Spread nut butter on each apple slice.
3. **Add Toppings:** Sprinkle with optional toppings if desired.
4. **Serve:** Enjoy as a quick snack or dessert!

www.ingramcontent.com/pod-product-compliance
Lightning Source LLC
LaVergne TN
LVHW081340060526
838201LV00055B/2770